AFTER THE SNAP

Kian A.Furnace

DEDICATION

This book is dedicated to those who start over.

ACKNOWLEDGEMENTS

I would like to thank my poetry sister Ronda TruFiyah Lloyd Peck. Having her read this book and challenge me to become a better poet was everything.

I also want to thank my mama and my father for telling me the truth during this period of transition. To my brothers Mikhail and my twin Roshia and his lovely wife Dachan they were my rocks during this time period. My sister-cousin Felicia Burnside (Frog),as she came to check on me to keep my spirits lifted during a low point. I appreciate each of your love and support.

Thank you, Tameka Forte for reading, and Jenna Mack for counseling and praying for me throughout this ordeal. I want to thank the "Love Jones," my soulful friends from Ohio who found me in NC and helped me curate not only my art, but other artists and lots of great music during this era.

To my good friend Chad Lockhart, thank you for your empathy and sharing some of the adventures on the road to recovery. To Kish McCray, Shannon Douglas and Zaria Davis Humphries, Tesha Lowery my Wilberforce brothers and sisters who held me down, thank you.

Now last, but certainly not least, to my beautiful wife ReShockie "My Nina", thank you for finding me, seeing me, and restoring me (more on her in subsequent writing <3).

FOREWORD

I was there before the snap, but my part as a sisterly companion on this journey would not be well written in until the "after." Before then I merely glanced at the pages of what I know now to be a perfectly imperfect masterpiece. The thing about K.Furnace is that he loves the art of speaking, or rather writing on love almost as much as he loves love itself. This is why in the coming pages you will find yourself completely drawn in... because that's what love does... It draws you in. Even when it's painful it still has a way of being compelling. Even when it's crushing, it never ceases to bare its beautiful side at the end. And this is why even once we've become casualties to its pitfalls, often many times over, we still find ourselves on the uncertain road that leads to Love.

The beautiful part is when we are fortunate enough not to have to travel the painful places alone. Insert "After the Snap." K.Furnace takes you on a journey of loving, losing and hoping to find. It is the sometimes bitter, sometimes sweet, poetic pouring of his own reality on the written page so that you may find healing or just know that you're not alone. His writing is sentimental, mellow, powerful, yet smooth; picture Common telling poetic lullabies in between sips of the finest cognac and you will sense the velocity of this work.

After the Snap is an ultra-transparent rending of a man's soul who has crossed love's dangerous terrain and made it to the other side. Therefore he can be trusted to curate you through your own journey of navigating love's painful parts. Whether you are reading for healing, pleasure, or simply because you love great poetry that is authentic and able to paint a clear picture, you have come to the right place. The words you will read after these will change you in ways that you won't expect, so get comfortable and take it all in. Beauty awaits... *After the Snap.*

TruFiyah

If Donald "Duck" Matthews and Julian "Murch" Murchison were morphed together, it would be YOU! This has been the running joke for the last 10 plus years, but I never really explained to you how I arrived at these 2 fictional characters. "Duck" has a DEEP love and passion for music and words. The way words are strung together. Their sounds, tones, textures. The feelings they give when read, sang and/or spoken. "Murch" has quiet confidence and is far more brilliant than he presents at times. He doesn't like conflict but isn't afraid to stand tall and strong for what he believes. When you shared your poetry with me years ago, to me, it reads like music. You cannot help but hear melodies and rhythms. I could hear so many different artists from different genres creating your words and bringing them to life. They would get to experience words and music in such a way that they would never look at the 2 the same again. Fast forward to 2020, the year of clear vision. My friend, my brother is sharing his gift with the world and I couldn't be more proud. All of those late nights and constant revisions, sharing your thoughts and dreams has manifested. The world will FINALLY come to know your gift in the way I have for over twenty-five plus years.

Ladies and Gentlemen, The New York Times Best Seller, Pulitzer Prize and Nobel Prize Literature Recipient...Kian A. Furnace. We're speaking these things into existence!
I. Tameka Forte' AKA Mohagany Brown

The heart has retired from the pendulum of pain... it now has a charismatic rhythm that beats with love and peaceful cadence. During his journey from elementary(he gave a speech at our 6th grade commencement) to his adult years, Kian has always been genuinely thoughtful and a wordsmith. If poetry had a freestyle competition, Kian would kill it. The stanzas, similes and imagery make me think of Nikki.

Going forward, I would love to end this foreword with complete adoration and celebration. He has inspired me to revisit my love for linguistics and romance. He is an inspiration to all who come in contact with him! I hope that you readers connect with the blessings that I have been blessed to hear for over 30 years.

Jenna King

TABLE OF CONTENTS

INTRODUCTION

In 2012 my world shattered in two. It was the beginning of the summer, and I received a phone call that my wife of 5 years had decided to leave me. For the better part of the spring we had toiled in a downward spiral toward our eventual demise. The news, in all honesty, was long overdue. In fact it was like a game of chicken; we were waiting to see who would blink first.

There were no kids harmed in the making of this breakup. I was tasked with starting over unprepared, brokenhearted, and 3 years shy of my 40 birthday. I was afraid and a little ashamed of being almost 40 with no kids, no wife, and was about to leave our marital home to become a bachelor again with a roommate.

Let me first say that under most life-altering changes like these you should consider some sort of therapy, and/or counseling. Even religious advice should be considered, in most cases, in order to gain some coping skills, understanding and perspective to help you not go crazy with self-doubt, anger or blame.

My poetry filled this void. I wrote steadily about my pain to distract my pain and to share my pain. Through my writing I have created a snapshot of this time in my life circa June 2012. My writing is an amalgamation of fear, self-doubt, regret, hurt, hope, and healing.

BOOK I:
ANTHOLOGY OF POEMS

Written After, During and Before

DUET

(I have no fucking clue) Robin Thicke final
2:32 of I Don't Know!

I don't know how it feels to be You…
But I also refuse to call something green when it's Blue!
You claim to hold on to this notion of the Truth
Whose?

The most convenient truth is lies
Hidden in plain View
We are losing time, patience
Hair, and gaining Weight.

You don't see my frustration, clothed in my apathy
Toward your viewpoint and the controversies your mind
Creates
It gets more and more confusing
Attempting to do and say all the right things even taking blame
for things for which I have no fucking Clue!

Inherent sensitivity and make believe skeletons
Too often you intrude, I interrupt, just too plain Rude!
Silence and indifference is my interlude, are we just ignoring
the elephant in the Room?

2

Neither one of us can hear each other when we Scream.

Her silence and distrust is inescapable even in my Dreams.

I try to not be rude, but I get tired, I Complain.

I come home to this every day.

I don't have the sense to come out of the Rain.

Today I got inspired while listenin' to Robin Thicke.

I uncovered that I'm not alone

No man knows what makes his woman Tick!

RE-UP (RE-FILL ELLE VARNER)

Can I re-up, double back

Hit my supply, my stash spot

Go to the well one more time?

I got you on my mind

I wanna get high

I am sitting here tripping 'cause I don't know

where the time has gone,

I feel like a stoner in my cartoon t-shirt Where is my bong?

'Cause my high is coming down, something's slipped my mind.

If I look I still won't find, 'cause I'm all out of love and of time.

Man, I could use a re-up.

Can I get a re-up?

I haven't smoked since college, but it feels like

I need to get high above the clouds.

I wanna make myself a sandwich, watch a little

TV, play my records too loud.

In comes reality, definition of insanity, life

and its routine, monotony.

I feel like the boy who is scraping change from the underside of

my seat Cushions or the ashtray of my car or change from

piggy, that's supposed to be for washing clothes.

I'm on empty, running out of gas, this
love can't go far
Until I get a re-up.
Can I get a re-up? Yeah!

SEEKING A FRIEND FOR THE END OF MY OLD WORLD AND THE TRANSITION TO MY NEXT... PART 1

The way you left should have given me pause.

Don't get me wrong I know we both were flawed.

There was always a trace of discontent; you

never even tried to throw me off the scent.

I guess it's part of your DNA to run

From your commitments.

As I look closer perhaps it was always imminent

You got demons, skeletons,

That closet door never got cleaned, or opened.

Instead I have these words in which I opined

To make sense of it all

Separate yours from ours

All that's left is y.

Since you seek space, now I see stars.

Now I must be a quick healer

No one likes to see open wounds and scars.

SEEKING... PART 2

Now I am seeking a friend for the end of my old world.

A true friend for the journey to repopulate,

Let's imagine I found a way to escape.

Toward the end things escalated, got real, *real* quick

Unfortunately, I never knew how sick.

I feel terrible and will until I have another crack at it.

A chance to do things much differently.

I'd talk less, listen more

Pray, Pray, Pray, reiterate pray

Involve the Lord

Make my intentions pure.

Protect her, like I'd never protected a soul.

Maybe then I'd have a hand to hold

As the world continues to spiral out of control

Around us.

JENNY (FRIENDZONE) PART 1

Frank Ocean, Forrest Gump, my version

I fell for those condescending cheers
You always confirmed my worst fears
That I'm your favorite pastime.

You are always on my mind
Yet I'm always standing in line
We're not talking speed skating either.
I'm always the bottom feeder
Getting what the others have left behind.

If I'm receiving the brunt of the neglect and
oversight and abuse
You made your life choice
For loving you I make no excuse.
Lovers you've had many, I haven't loved any.

Here I am waiting for you, as you return from seeing the world.
You will always be my girl, Jenny!
Even if you return worse for the wear,
I will be at your bedside as you close your eyes this final time
With a tear in each eye.

JENNY (FRIENDZONE) PART 2

Regrets there will be many,

What if you had taken the time

To come in out the rain

A life saved from immense pain.

Instead you chose to see the world

Live for today, fuck tomorrow.

My eyes still see you in that very first light

Like a puppy dog I follow.

You have me on a leash and I jump at your command.

As I became older and became a man

It became clearer where I stand.

Maybe you only see me in that friend zone.

I'm a man with needs

These needs run deep in my bones.

You see as I was running toward that end zone

I was pretending I was coming to save you,

making you my own.

THE ELEMENTS OF SUSTAINABLE LOVE

Earth in her care and consciousness,

Wind's flexibility, spontaneity, easy going,

positive, forward minded, demure, kind.

Fire which emblazoned a trail through her essence to mine

Through her excellence, hardened like refined silver

Aggressive, assertive, knows what she wants,

vigorous in her lovemaking

Tireless in her kingdom duties, convicted by her spirit and her

character.

Water, the true life source, sensitive enough

to share what pains she feels.

Real enough to not allow it to stop her—although

she may have to yield.

Cleanliness next to her godliness, her care for plants and

people and animals alike.

Love the hardest of the elements to find can't be synthetically

Created or bootlegged.

There is no magic potion.

Love, all encompassing, passionate, honest, true.

Elements like those of Earth, Wind & Fire.

If each of these elements exist in one being—and I believe they

do—

Then you'd not only have my devotion

I'd be in love with you!

BAD KARAOKE

#Friday Poetry moment

Sing like no one's laughing at me
Wondering what he go and do a
thing like that for.

After hearing all the hate directed
Towards unfazed by the jeering
You rose to your feet
Begging for more.

I can't front, this was so far out of
My comfort zone.
It just goes to show that I'd be
A fool for you.
Short of streaking down Tryon
It's a pretty short list of things I wouldn't do.

So I saaaang so loud and off key
My pitch and tone do not agree.
Can't be found in musical range
Some might find this strange.

Most wouldn't put themselves

Up for so much scrutiny

Subjecting themselves to humiliation

By bad karaoke.

EITHER OR

K Furnace Sunday Night Flow!

Either or
Sunrise or sunset
The close of a perfect day could be depressing
The end of a horrific one couldn't come fast enough
The promise of a new day or more of the same.

Winter snow makes it impossible to go outside
But could also have its charm
Two lovers with cabin fever quarreling.
Or hot cocoa, fireplace and movies
And nestled in each other's arms.

Here or there doesn't matter
See anywhere will do
Fall in Ohio, springtime in DC,
Winter back in Cali and summer
In love with you.

UP LATE WRITING

(Between a rock and a heart place)

I'm between a rock and a heart place
My head is spinning
Hit with flurries I'm on an island
In the center of a storm.

My mind is in a fragile state
I just want a clean slate
My current purgatory
Wiped away clean
I wanna awake to find it was all a dream.

I want to say I miss you
But that's not entirely true.
What I miss is more than you
More than you could provide
More of the stuff that's found inside.

The look in her eyes
More than her walk,
More in her way
Beauty found on the inside.
Resilient, natural, effortless

This breeze flows unpredictably

Vigorously, definitely.

No one likes to be alone

But I'd prefer to be in a lion's den

Than to spend another day with you

If you are not the one.

I heard them say divorce is a sin.

So is wasting time

On someone who you don't think of as friend

So we must brace ourselves for the end.

All this time gone by, all we did right was pretend.

Hey at least there are no kids involved,

Our one positive spin!

LOVE IN THE ABSTRACT PART 1

Love in the abstract,
A time for introspection
While on the intersection of life
I've wasted enough time.

Lost one wife
At the risk of sounding cliché
This is my cathartic way of dealing.
What I need is time to deprecate
It's in the DNA of my writing.

To describe altruistic, fairytale expectations of love
Life is full of setbacks and rejections, they say.
You'll hear no, a lot more than you will yes.
This is the incantation, you'll hear most analytics
Chant to talk themselves into insanity.

Don't talk me to death, incessantly or till my ears
Fall randomly from my head.
You drone on never realizing
I can't hear a word you just said!

LOVE IN THE ABSTRACT PART 2

I must be missing the forest for the trees.

Am I epidemically too naïve?

It is through my journey

I became totally free.

Gotta stop

Trying to connect

Every dot.

Some experiences are round trip

Some abruptly stop.

Thus the ride I've been on

Never reaching that crescendo.

A series of bad notes

Unlike those other blokes

I have the wisdom gained from such epic fails.

I glean understanding from where I made missteps

I look forward to setting sail.

The deep blue sea, sink into the depths

My sub selfishness, been trying to narrate

For too long, time to escape.

Where to? An island off the coast of my

Wildest dreams, fantasies, reality.

Setting new norms, while discovering the most breathtaking
forms
Where love was once frail, I pray she finds herself back to me
thick.
It's gonna be showtime all the time #Magic.
Not too much, never too little, or too high or too low.
Knowing my ceiling never reaching the bottom
The scales of my desires must be evenly weighted
what you expect when you're born in the autumn.

CONDITION OF MY HEART PART 1

Inspired by Prince

It does matter what shape they find me in.
Will I look downtrodden, sad or worried
Or happy with a grin?
Will I be slain, or die peacefully in my 80's?
Who will deliver my eulogy?

Who did I spend my last days with and how?
What did I eat? What did I wear?
Was there any foul play?
Did my former loves shed any tears?

What will be spoken of how I lived in the dash?
Did I suffer or go fast?
What will my friends say when asked
What kind of guy was he?
Did he live passionately?
Or did he live passively
Letting opportunity pass him by?

Did I ever become whole?
Or am I just the sum of a lot of unfinished and uneven parts
Which explains the concern over the condition of my heart?

CONDITION OF MY HEART PART 2

Was there an alternative ending
One where my demise would have been different?
Is any of this even important?
Did I receive a warning?
Have I already missed the alarm?

Was it someone close to me who did me harm?
Who am I survived by?
What did I die for?
Did I leave a legacy behind?

Will my deeds be forever remembered,
Favorably looked upon as a man who was
One of a kind?
Now that I'm finished will I be a cautionary tale
For everyone's life to start?
Or is this another life in passing
Over the condition of my heart?

In my afterlife will I receive the answers
To all life's great mysteries?
Will it be as important to me then
In the end?
What will matter?

Money spent, things scattered

Amongst family and friends, charity

Who felt my unwavering love, sacrifice?

Is heaven a destination or is it a part of the life

We share with each other on Earth.

What will be made of my art?

Will it be used as the final epithet

Memorialized eternally as the condition of my heart?

AMAZING TIMES

I'm living in amazing times.
I got unfiltered
Brutally honest rhymes.
My emotions broken down
In my gut like enzymes.

I tear my soul
While tossin' and turnin'
Over my misquoted notes
I am swerving unconsciously,
Uncontrollably unnerved by circumstances.
I find perspective in the cursory glances.

What am I supposed to do?
I'm just writing until you tell me not to.
I don't always say the right thing.
Am I predisposed to bad timing?
On this bus bad lighting
Bad weather thunder lightning
Frightening.
My letter to anyone who's listening!

BROKEN

Can you break something that's already broken?

With Pandora's box already open

You never know what is liable to happen

On the turbulent seas of love.

U might accidentally unleash

The kraken.

I'm out and I am open

Silent but I am spoken

Asleep till I am woken

Well put together yet I am

Broken.

HELLO, AUTUMN

(Inspired by Summer Soft, Eivets Rednow)

In the meantime, it's not enough
To mean well, late spring early
Summer meant hell.

Although I have the summer's heat
To keep from losing my mind, I lost weight
Then along the way embraced the loss of freight.
Not mine anymore to carry on my not-so-broad shoulders.

With loneliness afoot, I skipped right over autumn, bracing
myself for a winter most certainly colder.
I guess fall has a way of bringing the change we all need.

Today I celebrate the harvest season. As in the fresh oranges,
berries, and kiwi I feed.
The change in colors of the leaves
As the more distance I place between me and she.

LUCY

The great pumpkin caper...

I can be such a blockhead

I am a disillusioned legend of the fall.

I see myself kicking a winning field goal

But this bitch Lucy keeps moving

The ball.

POTUS AND FLOTUS, HAPPY ANNIVERSARY!

She Who Has My Back, Part 1

She who holds my hand

She who helps me with

The things I wrestle with.

She who brings life to this

She who brought to life my special gifts.

She whom I attract the curious stares

By women who want to be her

Men who wish they had her

They can never say they have.

She who draws my bath

After a long day of work.

She who has her own self-worth.

She never takes away

It is she who adds.

She who holds me down on all fronts

She who has my back.

LET'S NOT AND SAY WE DID

I'm just being open and honest

Pardon my being candid.

Some guys can be stupid.

Don't let a few bad apples

Ruin the bunch.

I know I'm the one

Call it a hunch.

Maybe a premonition.

Call it a promotion

Let's take this to the next level.

If you pump up the bass

I'll handle the treble.

EAT, PRAY, LOVE/THE GLOW IN YOUR SKIN

It is amazing how some people
Wear their troubles like a tattered
layer of covering.
Whatever it is they're hiding
the truth is, it comes out anyway.
Something about their dermatology,
suggests there's pain hiding with in
And it lies deep beneath the skin.
It lies dormant,
and awaits to represent.
Never in the most positive ways
rearing its ugly head, semi-often.

I find through meditation, a quick simple vacation,
some relaxation, and dedication.
You may find a route from your worst iteration
all the way to manifestation.

That is the moment I starting feeling like
I was enough.
A glow returned to my skin.
Attribution to my new mantra,
Eat, Pray, Love.

ON LOOSE LEAF PAPERS

On loose leaf papers
She was noted on
Beautiful love ballads
I was quoted on.

Every opportunity she will
Be doted on.
If my kiss was sugar
It would be coated on
This might be cloud #9
I floated on.

HAND HOLDIN'

Her presence in my world

I beseech

In hands, candy, and flowers

In each

Armed with good intentions

And sugary speech

I'm sweet!

Hand holdin' to keep you near

As I spray these pheromones

In your ear.

You are scented and I'm pretending

That my time is short

I'm banking on it being

In your best interest

To be lendin',

by the close of our date you'd be

the one spendin'

all your lovin' on me.

HOW WAS YOUR DAY?

It's amazing what you miss?
Perspective is a delightful thing.
I never played the sounding board.
Never too much for gripe sessions.
Never put too much time into listening.
Today a friend vented. And I listened.

Intentionally, uninterrupted, definitely partial
but adequately objective.
I do hope I was a help, sincerely.

See we are fairly newly acquainted.
My ink isn't dry yet on my formerly
Betrothed.

Maybe the glue that I hope seals me to a new love
Is created in times like these
Conversations like these.

Bad days, long drives, understanding,
Overlooking the stress to find a way to unburden oneself
By engaging the partner in a debriefing on one's tribulations.
I definitely understand, formerly not too willing.

33

YOU COULD HAVE A PIECE OF MY LOVE

You dumb b@!$#

But you celebrate celibacy

Punish potential suitors.

You can dress up this foolishness any way

Color it 50 shades of gray.

You can look but won't find

No matter how hard you try

Like LL, says I am that type of guy.

You're too stubborn to try,

You'd rather act like a lady and lose this guy.

YOU

You improve my mood

You add melody to my tune.

You light my way like the moon.

I prefer you, I'm with you

In spirit, in deed, in truth

Like that, in a real way.

Y-owe-u when you can have

All my love now.

Why save for a rainy day?

I'm from Cali, it never rains there anyway.

THIS JOURNEY WE ARE ON...

May find us in storms

Don't say I didn't warn.

I've spent days upon days

Melancholy, forlorn.

I've been up I've been down

I've worked from dusk

Till dawn.

My faith in God, my loving wife is

All I have to call on.

Things my POTUS might say...

WHO BLEW OUR FLAME OUT?

Where did all the time go

When did we know

Who was the first to know?

How did we end up here?

Indifferent, separate

Flame blew out, desperate

To find some sanity.

Just a little part of what used to be.

I am trying to peel the layers

Of leftover you off of me.

What a mess we made.

Looking at the photo album

Wondering when will the memories fade?

FOR THE BEST

For the rest of my life
the best I could ever tell myself
is it was a tie score
I will wonder incessantly, if I could have
done more.

Instead it's a lonely winter,
The will to go on wasn't in her.

I face this life alone
On my own.
Such a bitter pill to swallow
Why must love always be on
loan.

MAYBE SHE WILL APPRECIATE ME

When we go out tonight
I compliment your beauty.
I exhibit chivalry
Because I pay for food and wine
I don't expect booty.
Maybe she will appreciate me.

Wondering if you'll eventually just
take me for granted.
Just finished 5th date out
firm kiss on cheek planted.

Candlelit white tablecloth
should not be a doubt,
what my intentions are.
How many men still
open doors when you
enter his car?

MAYBE SHE WILL APPRECIATE ME CONTINUED...

We fall asleep late on the phone
show up for date and it's
flowers to your home.

The signs I show have to be
considered.
What will you do
with all the romanticism
rendered?

You can't ignore
What is this all for?

If we keep going out,
what will be will be.
If I keep spending my money
and time maybe she will appreciate me.

HOW WILL YOU REWARD?

Don't take my kindness

for weakness.

My shyness and my sweetness,

for a reason you don't take me serious.

Don't underestimate

my prospects as a lover.

You can't ignore the obvious.

Can I blame it on the wine,

If I lean in to kiss you on your cheek?

I've made up my mind, and it's time

we ascend to the peak.

I respect your virtue.

Don't want to seem a freak.

I'm gonna lean in,

In hopes of a kiss on the lips I can sneak.

What narratives will be concluded,

when you consider the kiss?

Is it something that will be rooted?

Cheered in your circles, or thought about with sobriety?

At the end of the day, will you appreciate me?

AVONDALE BOND BROKEN

(I STILL MOURN THIS FRIENDSHIP AND ITS POTENTIAL KAF)

We should never have stopped being friends.

This was not how it was supposed to end.

I'm sure you got wind,

of it and it didn't sit well with me either.

What was I to do? I had a tough decision to make.

I did it, it backfired and my life has been one challenge

after another.

Friends in one's lifetime are hard to come by, even harder

when you stop talking over something petty.

I heard you are getting married,

I hope he makes you happy.

No one deserves love, more than you do.

It hurts that I may never get to talk or see you.

I hope it will be appropriate to catch up down the road in a

few.

Reminisce after a spell, unpack the last five years in review.

I miss you, I miss those little moments with a woman.

Who once called me friend.

WAXING POETICALLY

If mother earth picked a mate
father time, it could only be.
For love's sake, they procreate.
Their love's child, is her beauty incarnate.

Your toys are the rainbows.
Scenic views, picturesque
landscapes, clear cascading
clouds adorn your skyline.

When you cry, it always rains.
When you fall in love the earth quakes.
Someone, somebody out there
Must have heartache to balance out.
Because you've been given so much

That when you and I touch.
Joining our lives, hearts, souls,
People are made well.
The lame can walk; the mute can talk.
The tone deaf harmonize like angels singing before the creator.
There's not much your essence can't do.

The proof is running waters from springs

giving way to waterfalls.

As robins fly over, cycling the growth of berries, dandelions,

and clovers. Your grace is amazing.

LOST SOULS

Travelin' aimless at the speed
Of lost love, easy come easy go.
Long gone is pride being afraid
Of losing you.

Wearing my heart on my sleeve in a sensitive way,
lends itself to having my heart broken and perpetually on the
mend.
Oh well back to the drawing board with my crayons and my
youthful naiveté.

I'll go drifting in the abyss
as love and I just keep missing each other.
I'm so unsuccessfully into you,
I'm usually the last to know.

By the time the curtains are drawn, you've moved on.
I'm left picking up the pieces.
At least I have the routine down to a science.
I'm a natural at it. Yes, I'm good at it.
Lost soul never finding a home!

GOOD GRIEF

The narrative of Charlie Brown. (Lucy)

"So you want to hold the ball still
so I can kick?"
As soon as I get close, you move it
I know that trick.

Lucy, sometimes you make me sick.
You need to quit.
Stop being such a hateful bitch.
"This time you swear you'll let me kick?"
I believe you, so I fall for it.

I take my position for my running start.
On my sleeve is where I wear my heart.
So mark, get set, ready, I'll go running towards.
I'm such a hopeful romantic, that I must be a bore.

Predictable but great guy at my core.
Maybe I'm finally gonna get what I was waiting for.
As the ball sails through the air
I can hear the crowd roar.

I need her to keep the ball still.

I'm too trusting I'm betting she will.

After years of trying it's gonna be my biggest thrill.

All the playing games I've had my fill.

Tired of falling for the okey doke.

Losing my footing falling head over heels.

My kicking this proverbial ball is real.

EDGAR KIAN PO: RAVEN

The best part of being a single organism

Is when the wind blows you can take flight.

Far too long I saw life through her prism.

No longer being a support role in my own features.

I'm going to be her leading man tonight.

I'LL BE IN LOVE ON CHRISTMAS

If this happens, so surreal
it all seems.
Right out of your favorite
holiday movie scene.

I'll be home, right in your arms
If only in my dream.
If I can only peek into the wrapping?
With your arms around me
it would be a beautiful thing
loves perfect timing.

I'd be all a glow, then you'd know
in other words they'd see me smiling.

GOT TO FIND A WAY

I've got so much to say,
Instead I'm in this rut.
All wordless and bound up.
Sentences, paragraphs, pages
I can't construct.
Only if I would erupt, then this blank page could fill up
I've never been this flaccid.

49

FIND ME (K.A.F.)

Find me free, not yet.

Collected, but scattered.

Everything in the

World that once mattered.

Gone away from me.

But save your sympathy.

I was in purgatory

Waiting for effigy.

I delivered no eulogy

On the day she left me.

BLAME IT ON MY HEAD AND
NOT MY HEART

Leaving you amid your many emotional needs

Not exactly my exit strategy.

Sometimes my snap rush to action precedes

More intelligent forecasting

As the green light in my mind tells me to proceed.

I am guessing it's my head telling my heart what to do.

My heart just wants the love to flow.

I tried my very best honestly to love you

There's just some places where love won't go.

So many warning signs, saying goodbye is the hardest part.

Charge my error in judgement to my head and not my heart.

FIRST OFF...

First thing this AM
Fresh off getting it in
In the gym.

It's a beautiful day in the AM
Thought I'd take a second to edify,
Glorify, magnify Him.

Thank you for making
For keeping me
Never forsaken
My heart right now
In a frozen state.

I lost my love in the golden state
I've got to find my imperial
Somewhere although I'm far from a Wilton place.

Love can take you on a trip.
Waiting on the Hilton
To bring up my one suitcase.

WHAT PROFIT...
WRITTEN NIGHT OF LOTTERY

What profits a man to gain the whole world

Yet lose his soul.

Since you left my world has spiraled

In turmoil, out of control.

To date again or not to date at all

A blue, melancholy is unavoidable

Regrets sure I've got some.

With this winning lottery ticket

What pain could I erase if won?

What profit? I'll tell you tomorrow.

GEESE LOVE U 4 LIFE

Geese are monogamous animals

1 mate they whole life

For better or worse

Till feathers fall off

Or become soaking wet.

Together making movements.

Ripples in the lake waters.

Natural selection, they just fit.

Oh well, maybe we are not

Geese for a reason.

Meant to fall in and/or out of love.

Which explains the season,

Why I feel like wading.

THIS YEAR CHRISTMAS CAME EARLY

This year more than anything
Store bought, online purchase
A piece of jewelry and a new purse.
I'm giving out a double serving of me.

I know for several years on the subject of romance
I took a hard stance never making time
Work is the other woman, excuse after excuse.
Other woman barely now gets a second glance.

It's hard putting in the time and effort to do all things.
It is said that you can't serve two masters.
So in recognition of the season, in the spirit of good tidings
I, being me, fully. I'm here a day earlier than expected.
I come bearing gifts.

I want to make up for all the times you've been neglected.
This love of ours is respected.
You are the why, and what I do this for.
That's why you are worth more to me than anything I could
buy in the store.

After opening up your presents
After the food, the family

I just want to relax in your presence.

Indulge in your essence

I vow to try to fulfill your every wish.

LIFE/LOVE

Life/love imitate art

Love separate from heart

Love definitely ends but when does it start?

Well does it dearly depart?

2013 FREE ME VERSE

Excuse me if I don't reciprocate

I'm not in the mood to overcompensate.

Of late I have had to deviate

The new year is a new me time to celebrate.

The old me is staying in 2012

Too bad she couldn't appreciate it.

Short on capacity, so fantastically we left on uneven placement.

Not gonna placate, don't mind the tactical adjustment

I'm bullish on your bullshit in 2013.

Reiterate, you shouldn't find this too unsettling.

You put up with a lot worse from those who we shall deem less

than Sincere.

What we have here is my new heart's order.

God loving me, love will just have to play the

background for now.

7 POUNDS

Time often heals all wounds
My heart tossed away like lost and found.
Love does not grow on trees, nor out of ground
I will have to hold my breath until
Love abounds.

It's important to have a mind that's sound
Pieces of me scattered around
The timing of it all astounds
Love is not flat, it's round.
Its weight is measured in 7 pounds.

A LITTLE SUNDAY JAZZ

Perfume so sweet...
Why is her perfume so sweet?
I'm buzzing like a bumble bee
For that anticipated nectar,
So heavily layered on thick as tar

Rich like pre-colonized Africa
Your heat like that of the Sahara
Your walk and way like footprints in concrete.

Permanent like tattoos, colorful, unique
Your scent lingers and permeates
It resonates, radiates, stimulates
Is it your honey, or the funny way you buzz right on by me?

No other's song could sing to thee words more beautiful to say
Than when words to pen and pad do meet.

The song is on the way
Then the smell, with my eyes closed to see
It's the scent of falling in love
That is why perfume is so sweet.

MY FLAME

Inspired by Bobby Caldwell's 1980 something hit.
Also Biggie's Sky Is the Limit

Like pulling two pieces of plywood apart.
Stuck together for a period of time.
When separated there will be pieces of me left over on you, and
you on me.

Granted our glue wasn't strong enough to join us together for
all eternity.
Who's to say who is to blame.
Plus, I don't want to play that game.
All that matters is both of us made it out. Mostly unscathed by
the flame.

My world up in smoke, we are both culpable, enough blame to
go around.
Devastated as I am, I can't escape the sound.
The walls coming down around me for years.
The wheels on our love stopped on the side of the road with a
flat tire.
What's immaterial and unimaginable is how we got to this
world ending fire.
Inside and out, uncontrolled, inextinguishable.

It's not very plausible how two people got here.

I will always have my regrets.

For this I burn a candle.

Perhaps our love was more than the universe could handle.

MY L OPEN LETTER TO HER

I'm saddened most days burdened by the way things ended
If there was an apology appropriate. A gesture impending
My knees bending.

Instead divorce imminent. This is not ok!
Never in my wildest dreams did I ever expect we to be me.
Makes me appreciate a time not so distant.
Instead I'm in this foreign land.

How did we end up on two separate sides of this thing?
I want answers this instant. But there's nothing more to say.
You stopped wearing your ring, I stopped caring.
Now there's no communication, we have no peaceful dealing.

A lot of hurt feelings. I don't know if it's true,
An acquaintance saw you and heard you diss me.
Those lips used to kiss me. We used to pray together
Lord help me. That rocked me to the core.

I guess I'll be on my Baisden.
I'm a has-been, and there's no more love in your heart.
Tonight I cry in the dark.
It's unfortunate we had to end this way.

KEEP CALM

Keep calm and keep loving me

Keep calm and continue to fall in love.

We interrupt your regular schedule

Of programs to introduce you to your destiny.

Keep calm there will be another love on the hour.

Or on the horizon.

PROXIMITY

Wherever you might be
I hope I have a chance to search
The world over for thee.
I'm in the middle of a do-over currently.

I pray for you, love sight unseen
Just about every night I see you in my dreams. Like this one...
I'm eating in a Denny's in a one traffic light town.
Suddenly the place clears out and there's no one else around.

You and I make eyes; I don't crap out no snake eyes.
In fact, all sevens.
As you go on about this and that, neither of us close to leaving
Unless its arm in arm. As we sip coffee so warm.

No matter where she comes from when she comes in.
Time is of the essence.
Patience is a virtue as I hold out hope for love so true.
Gotta have something to believe in
Hold on to.

Love wherever you might be,
I have a feeling from reading the tea leaves.
Love in close proximity.
64

I'm her biggest fan
She's my dream come true.
A lot of people are rooting for us
Before they even know you.

I may be starting over.
This time in hopes to win
I'm looking for my lover.

IF I EVER...

Get another chance
I will make the most of love
I will be celebrated, make a toast
for love.

I'm optimistic despite the haunting
Peculiarly missing a ghost for love
I already have this thing imagined
How great the opportunity.

If I can just get up the nerve
To tell you what I need.
I need you
I need you
My heart beats for you
Cut my veins I bleed for you.

I look out for the tea leaves I take heed for you.
I have a word to share with you, perhaps a cup of coffee with
my boo.
So I could sit across the table and stare at you.
To pledge my undying love for you
No other's love would ever do
I need you.

It would delight me

Surprise me, like candle light.

In the moonlight, 33 floors high.

At a piano bar gazing out at stars in the sky.

If I ever get the chance to make my dream come true.

I need you.

I need you. I love you!

SATURDAY NIGHT/SUNDAY VISIT

She so damn fine, playing damsel in the tight dress,

Or she is too fly in leather or leopard print.

She is breathtaking, taking me on a natural high.

She goes out her way to speak to me.

When in the neighborhood she drops by.

She leaves behind her handkerchief it has her lipstick stain and

I'm wondering why.

Was she leaving me a kiss, was it simply this? A sigh, a wish...

FREEWRITING

Firmly entrenched in the vices

of love.

I warmly recognized that it's love.

A peace came over me

Lord have mercy.

My cup runneth over

I'm swimming in the fresh waters

Of the brook.

It wouldn't take a second look

A love like ours is right out of

A fairy tale book.

SURELY, SURELY, SURELY

No I guess I won't be getting

Any children named after me

To grow up, I'm glad I waited.

Surely...

Divorce is hard, but I have comfort

Divorce is hard, but I have comfort.

Surely you jest, you can't be serious.

Seriously, your cerebral cortex must be deficient

Curious with the dearth of quality.

Male prospects, good luck finding a man this decent.

I admit luck with women is non-existent.

I made my peace for my mistakes

For those I repent.

I'm happy to seek a soul mate who

Will understand me and know what I meant.

One who fuels me up and refuels me after all my energy is

spent.

In one regard I'm at a loss,

Adrift in a solitude like no other.

Licking my wounds, taking inventory: one lost lover.

Painstakingly in rebuilding mode.

Is this a manifestation of bad karma, reaping what I sowed?

Today I breathe a sigh of relief.

I become relieved that I can escape with my life, nothing owed.

No children were harmed in the departure.

It just wasn't my time yet to be a father.

Repeat... I guess you won't be naming no children after me...

CAN I BE A VICTIM OF LOVE'S DOMESTIC VIOLENCE?

Physical romance upside my head loving me black and blue.

No one actually harmed while making this love, lots of hugging

and kissing you.

Beat me the hell up by your romance.

She knocks me off my feet. I'm in a trance.

I'm fearful for my life if I make her trust me.

She might wanna indulge fully.

Her love is d-bo, on my front porch it's a typical Friday.

Her love is my bully.

Domestic violence.

FE

"I Wanna Know" inspired this.

The last hoorah, no more sunsets, sunrises, moonlight walk spent
together.
What happened to our forever?
I wanna know.

A love cut down before it had a chance to grow
They say it's better to have loved...
Or so the cliché goes
All the time invested
With nothing to show.

I tried playing the blame game
That just makes it worse.
I'd be lying to myself
If I said I didn't see this ending in divorce.

Those mind games that you play
Became par for the course.
This unfulfilled union I tried to forge.
At best divided, and forced
Two different paths, divergent and forked.
One day she's gonna realize what she had.
Then she'll be fucked.

SLEEP DEPRIVED

I miss being held tightly
Swiftly, thusly as the wind chill
Dips.
Routine, teeth brushed, peck lips
I miss this, nightly.

As winds of change leave us on opposite ends of our history.
I saw a couple in a movie that reminded me of us.
You tossing and turning, droning on about the last thing that
was on Your mind trying not to worry. Me trying not to fuss.

No matter how uneasy, or weary, or fraught with anxiety.
A good spooning would always offer needed sobriety.
You seemed to have a hold on me, until you decided to let go.
I now sleep alone on both sides of the bed on both pillows.

FREEWRITE PITY PARTY

Why am I here
In the wilderness alone?
I'm working without a net here
The world is wireless
I'm dial up-no net gear.
I have no gear
I had exit strategy
I wasn't prepared.

At star-crossed lovers
I stare with my eyes crossed.
Indulge me on my woe is me shit
If there is a rock bottom this has to be it.

What have I become?
It's so hard to stay positive
When you are lonesome.
Does spring bloom? Hope float?
Can I grow some? Soon before an entire year goes by.
Scorched earth dry.
Intensified by the lingering feeling of melancholy highs and
deep lows. Just thinking, drinking, praying while on my red cup
blues—solo.

THE CURE

Crazy set of circumstances left me exposed and vulnerable.
What was supposed to be unbeatable was waiting many nights
at the Kitchen table naked.
In full retreat mode secretly I'm in denial, like I could've done
more.
I was under prepared for the type of attack my relationship
would undergo. Straight up psychological war.
Now closing in on a year since she left, neither one of us
operates at our optimal. We were stripped down to the naked
truth, alone inside our truth that was so primal.

Imagine awakening to a fire set ablaze, uncontrollable. My
Phoenix and Her boundless energy cease to be as I prepared
for you to leave me.
Can one ever truly prepare for a tornado, hurricane or other
natural disaster? No amount of assurance is solace enough for
the injured.
My emotions range from "she got some nerve" to "maybe this is
what I deserve."
Now I'm in a place where I just want to recognize me, and I
hope not to recognize her as who we were when we parted
ways in opposition to who we could be.

I reconcile my time and my mission was completed. Still those sharp set Of circumstances pierce me at night and haunt me in my dreams. Not easily deleted. Cracks in heart enough to let the sunshine beams

Through photosynthesis I'm hoping to reach my proposed heights.

Though I may suffer, I endure.

As I look back on my journey I sojourn, while facing my truth. I may come up with the vaccination, treating the symptoms or inventing The cure. For a broken heart!

WATER

Lauryn Hill Unplugged (Kian breakfast in bed)

I shouldn't spend so much time in the forlorn
Saddened by the mistakes that haunt me
The past for which I cannot change is gone for good
Rinsed down the drain.
And that's a good thing.

A filtration system meant to recycle in
The fresh experiences and insights that will
Quench my thirst.
I wasn't the last and I won't be the first.

Love is a lot like water, or a running spring,
Or maybe a well
Time will tell if this levy will break again,
If my heart bursts open it could become a tsunami,
The epic disaster would be immeasurable
Carnage that devastates all who cross the path.

The pain is palpable, disease is incurable,
The number of affected people
Is a toll, that is non-billable.

YOU DO THE MATH.

The water I speak of can be a stream in a meadow,
It can be redirected as she could be swimming
Upstream with a different fellow.
My heart is yellowed, afraid of this angry sea,
Mighty storm torrential rain before me.

Never mind that I can't swim,
Couldn't save you if I tried,
Besides, who can swim and cry?
I've drowned in my failures drifting along

UNTIL I FOUND THIS LIFELINE

Now it's a combination of destiny and time.
Will I beach at a paradise or beaten by the rocks while floating
downstream. Sublime.

The water is a force, the beach beckons, can't have earth sans
water. Can't have food, can't have rain, can't have showers,
baths, soak pain Away, rinse away, drink to cure, can be serene
and pure.

Visceral, Celestial, natural, perennial, preferential, moving
about my earth Directing my new flow. Cleansing me, letting it
all go taken away lost in Your ocean living off the idea that
inside me will one day again grow.

AM BARS!

Socially conscious the new sexy

Imagine seeing out of your third eye

Knowing the questions, the answers, the reasons why.

Lately what's vexing me

Is the hunger games society preying on its young

Can't pray in schools

Kids play with guns

Leaving after 9th grade grown in physical

So underdeveloped in soul and spirit.

Hypnotized by misogynist lyrics

Devils conscripts, almost a script followed

Exact over 400 years, mighty mystics humbled

Demurred and docile.

Meanwhile we got a national Debate.

I wonder if our prayers reach the head of state

Now he wears a black face, but so do they!

Socialized health care, socially devoid of faith, socially fucked

Socialized networked society, trending topic.

Psychologically, sociologically fucked!

BROKEN

Reprint – Luther's I Who Have Nothing

I who am broken

I who have spoken too soon

As I now have no one

It's now a year in June.

I have been lost deserted

Adrift in a sea of my own emotions.

I'm intermittently frenzied to frozen

Numb to the reality of my shattered heart.

This was a clean break, no soft tissue fracture.

Who will help me pick up the pieces?

That is going to be the hardest part.

I who've been knowing

I who, can't tell if he's coming or going.

They look at you with sorrow in their eyes

More like that poor poor man.

They can see the sadness inside

They can read as my pen just cries.

I couldn't pretend anymore

No amount of sedative can conceal these lies

Now that the world knows, and can have a good laugh at me

I lay broken on this tiny apartment floor, disgusted at

what I see.

I without a home

I have a roommate but he lives alone.

I'm conspicuous to the eyes as her absence is my alibi.

I who have regretfully

I who contextually have replayed our final hours in the

Can't go back to the time machine that haunts me in my mind.

This kind of torture is what blurs the line

Between the living and the dead.

This is too much pain and suffering for mankind.

I who if I saw you tomorrow

Would have so much to say.

I who wondered what I could have done

to make you stay.

I who on my knees do pray

For your successful recovery

Run from all your demons and if any of them are me

Or your ability to love completely

Heal your mind free your body

I hope this time away gives you the perspective

Peace and serenity.

I have nothing more but my deepest apology

I lay broken in my own apathy.

SPIN

My spin on life

If you stick around long enough

Things will eventually work out.

My sin in life is I may not

Recognize the signs the first go round.

If I make it to heaven will I get the benefit of doubt?

In my next life will I author thoughts profound

Now that would be hot?

If I could invent something like the internet

I could find a cure for most things.

Imagine being able

To help human being's new wife

Champion the cause of humanity

These accomplishments would pale in comparison

To my nightmare to end my first life.

My subsequent separation and detachment from my first wife.

Waiting on number two, the start of

Those lifetime achievement honors

Receiving my Nobel, and thanking my inspiration of love.

In love and war all is fair.

On a destination to cloud #9

Are we almost there—just in time!

I could remember thinking how it all ended too fast!

Simultaneously another story is being told.

I remember reaching my hands to the sky

Telling the clouds, At Last!

UNCHAINED

When I make it out of here alive

A miracle I'll survive

I lived to fight another day

I'll never live in yesterday.

Forward my wings will heal

Another lost moment

Never again will she steal

I'm gonna swim upstream

In the river I cried

I no longer live in that lie

That part of me has died.

One day this will all be a memory

One day you'll see

The best part is yet to come

Love will return to me.

5150

Order can't be restrained

My love can't be contained

What we have can't be explained

Some might even say strange.

My world was turned upside down

I'm forever changed.

The ups the downs

The ins and outs

I have no pause or doubts.

It's crazy it's unstable

Then again so are we.

Flying by the seat of our pants

Call it what you will

Others want to call us names

Peace just won't be still

They won't let us chill

People wonder what's our deal.

They want to bring in the white coats

Take us to the 8th floor

Fill us with their medicine

Tell me we can't see each other no more

Unless we tell them why we are so crazy in love.

They want our secrets, they want our looks

Our giggles, our touch, they want to extract

They say they want to borrow

They won't give it back.

True love is to the bone like marrow

It's to the padded rooms for us two.

They can beat me black and blue

I'll survive 'cause the promise of our love will get me through.

No drug can be prescribed

No upper or downer

I'm already high.

My mood is altered by the mention of her name

I know she feels the same

We will be together again real soon.

She finishes the lyrics on our loony tune!

KIAN'S SILVER LINING PLAYBOOK

I thought it naturally

Celestial greetings

From birds chirping

Sweet smelling you

Greeted by smiling, happy you.

I can't help but feel like love cheated both of us

Not every story has a heroin who

Saves the day.

Some stories are devoid of a happy ending

I'm trying to find my silver lining.

At first I cried myself to sleep

Playing the what if game

That's one you can't win

Can't look back

Gotta learn to forgive.

I was willing to sacrifice my happiness

In order to give, give, give.

Can't squeeze blood from a turnip

I kept waiting for a breakthrough

But one never turned up.

So a year has passed

No sign of you

Time is moving fast
Perhaps in a vacuum.
I have sucked away your scent
No more perfume
I have yet to cast
Away all those demons
Perhaps the voices in your head
Talk to me too.

I hope I meet someone who
Makes me just as crazy
In love too!
To me that would be winning
It would be my silver lining.

SUMMER'S REPRISE

Not yet out of spring
Not yet out of that thing.

In late May of 2012
I affectionately call that my personal hell.

I live another four seasons
I have yet to find my reason.

In the passing of yet another year
I haven't found things more clear

In fact I'm pensive
Reluctant to give.

My heart hopes and it dreams
At night I awaken myself with loud screams.

Sometimes replaying those episodes in late May
Wondering if I would go about things a different way.

THE SPIRITUAL STREAM

Somewhere in the Universe is every answer we want to know

Our personal responsibility is to

Explore cosmic consciousness

Along with the disclosed and undisclosed.

The Universe has seeing eyes, the orientation is seen from

earth mostly at night.

The picture is truly developed when we stop obscuring the

environment

with artificial light.

The Universe is an entire space and time continuum—

A steady flow of consistent inconsistent

Intelligent in design, yet purposely

Interim.

PERSPECTIVE

It's a matter of orientation

How close one is to the sun

It's a matter of opinion

Who left with less scars

Measured in who lost or won.

I'D BE OPEN FOR THAT...

But she might have some soul searching going on.

Instead all we have is my thoughts forlorn.

Meanwhile if you get caught out there and you realize the truth

No, a piece of you will always be attached to me like glue.

After all, I will always love you.

My soul is free and karma clean.

No malice at heart, from my point of view.

I WOULD IF...

I would if I could roll back the years
I would simply hold back the tears
I would pin back the ears
I would clip away the thorns
With my shears.

It was just a blur
I blinked and you weren't there
Frightened standing in the dark
You could smell it in the air
We were supposed to trip the light fantastic
I was gonna be like Fred Astaire.

What happened was a comedy of errors, poor judgement
And an opportunity taken advantage of.
It's what happened when she stopped caring and pretending
she was in Love.

I'm in my lonely place banging away at my computer keys.
One year and a day from where she left me.
Am I worse for the wear, most noticeably?
Am I carrying on as if love will one day abound right here
beside me.
Most definitely.

I would if I could roll back the years

I would simply hold back the tears

I would pin back the ears

I would clip away the thorns

With my shears.

BEFORE I EMBARK...

Before I embark on the green way toward enlightenment

Sweet vermouth and dry

Add the bitters.

Hard pill to swallow

Especially when I didn't quit her

What happened and why is im-material

For the better part of the year even now

Rendered im-mobile

Mixing my bleeding heart with rugged optimism

Cause I'm-smooth.

Mixing reality with what helps me sleep.

Looking in the mirror

'Cause it's truth

No amount of tonic water can dilute.

Can't distill heartache

Be still my heart

Can't fake

Not on real emotions.

Not even the ones that appear in phone text

Or on Facebook post

My pain has dwelling inside me,

It's a daily dinner party

And I'm the host.

SHE MOVES ON FIRST

I have prayed for her grieving
Thinking she might be mourning me
Till one day I did a search on FB and was
surprised to see.

At first glance a couples' picture under a tree
I was floored by the intimacy.
They looked in love, I was pierced deeply
In the core of my belly.

I guess I have a revisionist view of history.
That's when I discovered I was praying for her misery
Not her recovery, the big thing for me to do is to wish her to be
happy.
Instead I was keeping her in my own memory, deep, dark,
sullen, a prisoner of our unholy ending to our matrimony.

It's so phony, so not sweet, so not sincere, so selfish of me.
When I give my prayer to God it's for her total recovery, even if
it had to come at the expense of me.